Date: 5/10/18

Feeling Sad

by Rosalyn Clark

LERNER PUBLICATIONS ◆ MINNEAPOLIS

Note to Educators:

Throughout this book, you'll find critical thinking questions. These can be used to engage young readers in thinking critically about the topic and in using the text and photos to do so.

Lerner Publications Company
A division of Lerner Publishing Group, Inc.
241 First Avenue North
Minneapolis, MN 55401 USA

For reading levels and more information, look up this title at www.lernerbooks.com.

Library of Congress Cataloging-in-Publication Data

Names: Clark, Rosalyn, 1990— author.
Title: Feeling sad / by Rosalyn Clark.
Description: Minneapolis : Lerner Publications, [2017] | Series: Bumba books. Feelings matter | Audience: Ages 4–7. | Audience: K to grade 3. | Includes bibliographical references and index.
Identifiers: LCCN 2016054407 (print) | LCCN 2017004810 (ebook) (print) | LCCN 2017004810 (ebook) | ISBN 9781512433678 (lb : alk. paper) | ISBN 9781512455472 (pb : alk. paper) | ISBN 9781512450279 (eb pdf)
Subjects: LCSH: Sadness in children—Juvenile literature. | Emotions—Juvenile literature.
Classification: LCC BF723.S15 C53 2017 (print) | LCC BF723.S15 (ebook) | DDC 155.4/124—dc23
LC record available at https://lccn.loc.gov/2016054407

Manufactured in the United States of America
1 – CG – 7/15/17

LERNER e SOURCE™

Expand learning beyond the printed book. Download free, complementary educational resources for this book from our website, www.lerneresource.com.

Table of Contents

Feeling Sad

Sadness is a feeling.

It is okay to feel sad sometimes.

When have you felt sad?

Maybe you moved to

a new neighborhood.

You left behind good friends.

This made you feel sad.

Maybe it is a rainy day.

You can't play outside.

This makes you feel sad.

You might feel left out.

Maybe your friends are ignoring you.

Maybe your team lost a game.

Losing can make you sad.

Why would losing a game make someone feel sad?

Maybe your pet died.

You miss your pet.

You might cry when you are sad.

It is okay to cry.

What other things might you do when you feel sad?

16

Sadness is a strong feeling.

Everyone feels sad at times.

Talking to friends or family can help.

Sometimes your friends may feel sad.

You can ask if they are okay.

Talking to you may help your friends feel better.

What can you say if a friend is feeling sad?

Picture Quiz

Which child is sad? Point to that picture.

Picture Glossary

feeling

an emotion or thought

ignoring

not paying attention to something or someone

neighborhood

an area where people live

team

a group of people who work together to play a sport

23

Read More

Hibbert, Clare. *I'm Sad and Other Tricky Feelings*. Mankato, MN: Amicus, 2011.

Kawa, Katie. *I Feel Sad*. New York: Gareth Stevens Publishing, 2013.

Orr, Tamra. *Sadness*. Ann Arbor, MI: Cherry Lake Publishing, 2017.

Index

Photo Credits

The images in this book are used with the permission of: © Belinda Pretorius/Shutterstock.com, pp. 5, 23 (top left); © Konstantin L/Shutterstock.com, pp. 6–7, 23 (bottom left); © TinnaPong/Shutterstock.com, pp. 8–9, 22 (bottom right); © praetorianphoto/iStock.com, pp. 11, 23 (top right); © asiseeitt/iStock.com, p. 12; © Africa Studio/Shutterstock.com, p. 14; © michaeljung/Shutterstock.com, p. 17; © valbar/Shutterstock.com, p. 18; © Lordn/Shutterstock.com, pp. 20–21; © FangXiaNuo/iStock.com, p. 22 (top left); © iStock_Oles/iStock.com, p. 22 (top right); © MaFelipe/iStock.com, p. 22 (bottom left); © FatCamera/iStock.com, p. 23 (bottom right).

Front Cover: © 3dvin/Shutterstock.com.